Seriously Now, Enough Already

Daphne Leigh

WESTBOW
PRESS®
A DIVISION OF THOMAS NELSON
& ZONDERVAN

WestBow Press books may be ordered through booksellers or by contacting:

WestBow Press
A Division of Thomas Nelson & Zondervan
1663 Liberty Drive
Bloomington, IN 47403
www.westbowpress.com
1 (866) 928-1240

Scripture taken from the King James Version of the Bible.

ISBN: 978-1-9736-1438-8 (sc)
ISBN: 978-1-9736-1437-1 (e)

Print information available on the last page.

WestBow Press rev. date: 01/11/2018

Contents

Foreword

I f there is anything I want the public to take away from my writings it is the understanding that we serve a mighty, faithful God. I am a person who was born with numerous challenges, and those challenges have followed me through my life. What has followed me as well is the grace and mercy of God. My previous book, Life Overcomer, talks of dealing with these challenges growing up and how they affected my life. It also details how God has set me free! God can take the word "disability" and change it into the words "great ability".

Life has changed for me a lot since I finished my first book and I have gone from being a career woman to being mostly retired because of disability issues. So here I am in my favorite chair wrestling this notebook and pen away from my two cats. I will also be learning how to use a voice activated computer program as these two hands of mine can no longer do much keyboarding. The past fifteen years have presented many challenges as well, more than I can even believe. I realized after completing my first book that I ended the story just when it was really getting good. So "Seriously Now, Enough Already" continues on with the last fifteen years of my life, experiences lived, and lessons learned along the way.

You might think the title of this book a little odd. The truth is that life happens, people are not perfect, relationships are very hard work and yes, even the cats I love so much occasionally will throw up on my (white) furniture, or God forbid, on my bed! (Yuck!) In all the good, bad and ugly of life God is there, he is faithful, and in the midst of our hurt and confusion He loves us so much. He has taken me through so much. He asks us to trust him enough to walk through life one day at a time, holding his hand. And when we can no longer walk through it, he is there to carry us. The one truth in this world that will never change is God's Holy Word. Jeremiah 29:11 reads "For I know the plans I have for you declares The Lord, plans to prosper you and not to harm you, plans to give you a hope and a future."

It is my hope that "Seriously Now, Enough Already" will make you laugh, and make you cry – as the last bit of life has done with me, and to help us learn these lessons in life He has for us all. Lord bless and keep you.

Acknowledgments

$\mathcal{I}$ want to thank those people in my life for their constant support as I work on this book. Mom, Dad, Sisters and Brothers, your influence in my life has helped to shape me into the person I am today. Christian Family, your support and prayers have watched me grow from my first wobbly steps as a new Christian at age 21, and have helped and loved me through each experience in life. You have never shied away from speaking hard truths to me and for that I am thankful.

My group of editors from my Home Group consists mostly of retired school teachers. Gang, this mission would be Mission Impossible without your help and support.

And for all the others God brings along the way, thank you, thank you and God bless you. It does take a village of committed, faith filled people to complete a project like this. May God bless it and help it to encourage others.

Coming Into My Own

My name is Daphne and I am a person who loves God, loves life and loves others. It's not that I bounce out of bed in the morning ready to tackle life, even if I do love sunrises. My morning routine, which includes core work and stretching and toning to Christian music, does its job to change my attitude from tired and grumpy to encouraged and thankful for another day. I do the core work because I am determined to have one area of my body which is strong. The stretching and toning is physical therapy for the other areas of my body which need help. I was born with some challenges, and also have had injuries which have happened over time. I'm not always excited to get into my morning routine mind you, but feel so much better after I get it done. I'm always glad I did it. So here's my secret. If you let your mind wander to something besides what you are doing at the time, you will not be thinking about the torture you are putting your body through!

My life has been all about meeting challenges head on. As we all know, even the loveliest roses of all have some thorns. The challenges I have faced affect me both physically and developmentally. I was plagued by severe learning disabilities both in school and on the job. Life was anything but easy. In my first book, Life Overcomer, I tell the story of the long road which led me to God, to healing and to wholeness, and how learning of a treatment called Vision Therapy helped to free me from my learning challenges. There was so much to overcome back then! When I finished that manuscript in 1998 I was still completing my Vision Therapy treatment and with the help with these good people I have gotten the learning challenges and dyslexia somewhat under control. Life had gone on and has been good. I found myself in my eighteenth year working at a beautiful Christian University in Seattle, Washington and living in an amazing apartment across from the Campus. I had a job that balanced data entry and customer service, and found a way to make it work. I loved my Church and worked very hard at Music Ministry and Children's Ministry. I had moved into worship team ministry and played my guitar and sang with the team each Sunday morning. I had rock-solid relationships with good friends and mentors.

My Vision Therapy work had really helped me in my job to bring down a very high margin of error due to a naturally dyslexic brain. It is not easy to hold down a highly technical job when you have learning challenges. Sometimes it seems nearly impossible. I had to learn to find ways to compensate for my challenges, and most difficult of all, learn how to forgive myself for not being perfect. As time went on I found more and more tools I could put in place to help with accuracy at work. I needed to walk into work daily with an "I can do this job" mentality and belief. The encouragement of those around me reinforced this mindset and I could rest in the routine I had put together to help myself do my best. One of my favorite scriptures of all time is Psalm 37:3-6. "Trust in the Lord and do good; dwell in the land and enjoy safe pasture. Delight yourself in The Lord and he will give you the desires of your heart. Commit your way unto The Lord; trust also in him and he will do this: He will make your righteousness shine like the dawn, the justice of your cause like the noonday sun." Life is good – the stage is set. Now for the next fifteen years of life.

Fourth of July Story

I remember the first time I experienced July 4th in the little penthouse apartment I lived in for four years across from my University Campus. It was on the side of a hill and then had a decent sized outdoor stairwell to my front door. I was high enough up to have a lovely territorial view of the area. I could sit outside in the summer on my large private deck and watch the boats coming and going along Seattle's ship canal. I could look to the East to see the cars traveling the I-5 freeway and I could see the Cascade Mountain Range behind it in the distance. This little place was such a refuge for me during the times when my job was extremely stressful.

Well, on that first Fourth of July, the fireworks experience was something to behold. After the sun set I heard all this commotion outside and I opened my front door to see what was going on. Oh My! The fireworks show set off at Lake Union was right in front of me! I ran out on my deck to enjoy the rest of the show. The Lake Union fireworks show was close enough that it felt like I could reach out and touch it. I remember thinking "Next

Summer I simply have to share this with the people I love." And so I started making plans for next years Fourth of July bash out on my deck. As my private deck was built over the second story of my apartment house and supported by the apartments below me there was no danger of a deck collapse, and I was thankful for that. The end of June the next year saw me making up some fliers for the fireworks party and passing them out at Church. As my home was near the heart of downtown Seattle and my Church was in Mountlake Terrace, a suburb to the north I really didn't know what kind of response I would get. I planned the party food and planned to have plenty of it.

My friends and their kids began to arrive that afternoon. It was a perfect day and I remember doing my best to talk the little boys who came out of scaling my deck's railing and hanging out on my downstairs neighbor's roof. It was a huge draw for them. Towards evening the food was ready and out, and the people came. And came. And came. My place was full and the party was spilling out onto the deck. Everyone was enjoying the boats on the ship canal and the beautiful summer breeze.

Then the phone rang, it was one of the young guys from the youth group. They had spent the day swimming in his parent's pool and now he wanted directions to the party. As I hung up the phone I was in a sheer panic. I looked at my friends and said, "The youth group is coming…I don't have enough food!" They had been spending all day swimming and I knew that they would be hungry. I had a large bag of pretzels so I grabbed out a bowl and poured them in. I pulled out whatever else I had and added it to what the other people had brought. When the youth group arrived the guys offered to pool their money and drive up the hill for pizza. I was saved! The guys returned with the food just as the fireworks show began. And what a show it was! The gang stayed until about 11:00 PM to let the traffic die down some, and we all enjoyed watching the lights from the evening dance on the water. Finally it was time for the party to break up and for the people to head home. Poor dears… in the holiday traffic it took most of them two hours to navigate a commute that would have normally taken them 30 minutes! Needless to say, as fun as my party had been, the entire gang decided that they needed to stay closer to home when July Fourth came the next year.

University Mom

*C*ustomer Service was the favorite part of my work day. I remember years before when I first moved into this aspect of my job, the Business Office at our University would give out those chocolate coins covered in foil wrappers to students who came in to make tuition payments. I figured that if they could be the chocolate coin people then maybe I could be the candy lady! I talked to the Controller of the University about the possibility of me doing a monthly Costco run to pick up candy for the office and the receptionist desk, and any other supplies we needed. Then I filled out a reimbursement request to cover the expense. This, of course, made me quite popular around the office! As the floor receptionist it was my job to hand out paychecks, help route paperwork for the Departments, handle incoming calls and give out free candy. It was really fun to have exposure to a lot of the Campus, help them find their way around the paperwork issues and connect with people.

Our Students at the University many times found work-study jobs working in various Departments on our

Campus as they continued their schooling. I would see the Freshmen come in looking for paychecks and a piece of candy, but also looking lost and homesick, trying to adjust to college life. I had a real desire to reach out to these kids. I can call them kids because in reality I was old enough to be their Mother! I had a desire to be one familiar face that these students could come and see, get a paycheck and candy along with a smile and a "How are you?" I thought one thing I could do to make them feel more at home was to try and learn their names. Now this might seem like a mighty task when you hand out six hundred or more paychecks every other week. It was all about connecting the name with the face. So I made it into a little game. It was so fun to see their faces when they said their last name for their paycheck and I remembered their first name. Or when I saw them walking toward my receptionist desk and I had their paycheck out of the check box before they had signed for it or said their name. Trust me after four years of paying these great young people every other week you get to know a lot of students. By the time they graduate you are old friends, asking them about their future plans and you are really sad to see them go. But then Fall comes again and you have a brand new group of freshmen students to get to know, to be an encouragement to and to give free candy to!

One of our students loved Tootsie Rolls. She would come up for a paycheck and then take some Tootsie Rolls to put in her pocket – you know... a big test to study for and all. She came to be known by my Department as the "Tootsie Roll Girl" and I came to love her visits.

Well, graduation time hit at last for Miss Tootsie Roll. I remember being at one of our Campus wide graduation events and striking up a conversation with a woman sitting next to me. She had flown into town to see her daughter graduate from the University. You guessed it – Miss Tootsie Roll's Mom! Apparently Tootsie had gone to the airport to pick her up. As they were leaving Miss Tootsie reached into her pocket, pulled out a Tootsie Roll and popped it in her mouth, saying "Thank God for the Payroll Counter!" We all laughed about that for a long time.

There was also a more difficult side to handing out paychecks. If there was a paperwork glitch there was not enough information to be able to process the student's check. This sometimes led to a lot of frustration and emotion. I remember one student's reaction to hearing that his first paycheck was delayed because of incomplete paperwork. There was an immediate explosion of anger and shouting. I calmly directed him to the next counter over to check with the Student Payroll Technician and get the paperwork problem fixed. There was more shouting as he walked across the room to find the answers. After the promise of a rushed paycheck when the missing paperwork was in there was another burst of anger. He slammed the door open against the wall on the way out. Then I heard him proceed to fall down the steep stairwell as he exited our office, saying his angry words with every step he fell down. Then there was complete silence. Quietly I tiptoed over to the window to make sure I didn't need to call our Security Department and get this young guy some medical help but there was no sign of him. I hoped that as he hobbled off he was considering signing up for an anger management course!

It was really wonderful to become part of these students University experience. In time the Payroll Department opened up the opportunity to have paychecks direct deposited into the student's bank accounts. Though I was sad to see them less I was glad that this new policy would make their lives a little easier. I told these students that I would still be here at the payroll counter for conversation and free candy.

New Home, New Car

————— ⊙ —————

So time goes on, life goes on, seasons change. Something funny was happening in the winter of 1999. I was living in my wonderful penthouse apartment next to my campus. You know – all windows, big private deck, beautiful view. Because it was tiny the landlord kept the rent low enough to be affordable. But it was weird – it just didn't feel like home anymore. It felt the Lord speak to my heart that he wanted to bless me. So I wondered what that meant – what would happen?

In February of that year my parents were able to sell the office building that they had owned and managed for many years, allowing my Mom to finally retire. They invited me over for dinner and to talk. The first thing that they offered was to help me a little with a down payment on a new car. As I thought about this, my Dad pulled out a newspaper article about how banks were now looking for stable employees who had longevity at their jobs, to make first time homeowner loans with low down payments. They wanted to help me buy my first home! What a shock! As we talked about this, I was initially concerned.

How could I afford car payments and a mortgage on my salary? I also had some credit card debt I needed to pay off. But somehow God made a way. My parents knew that this would stretch me financially and promised to help me out until I found a way to make things work.

The plan still seemed a little crazy but we went car shopping and I found the right car. Then I talked to a friend from my church who sold real estate, a father to one of my good friends. We started looking at properties. Some good, some bad, some absolutely beautiful. You who have bought homes know how stressful the real estate process is. My income was not the highest but because I had stellar credit I was able to pre-qualify for a home loan under my name. Again, God had made a way. He had a plan. One place we looked at was really wonderful, and the homeowner had done a lot of work to update it and beautify it. The only drawback was that it was on the third story of the building and had three flights of stairs outside. I was already having issues from the knee surgeries I had as a teenager, and my Dad was concerned about me on all those stairs. But I really loved the condo we were looking at and I wanted to make an offer. We ended up in a bidding war for this condo – and lost. I'm so glad now that we did.

My Dad had seen a newspaper advertisement about a new building development in north Lynnwood that sounded interesting. My real estate agent, Dick, had heard of it too so one evening we drove there to check it out. At first I wasn't so sure about this property. It was quite far out north and I was thinking about a long commute to work near Downtown Seattle. I really wasn't ready to consider it, but Dad and my agent were persistent about going there one more time during the day to check it out. As we walked the property I started to feel a little better about the area. We checked in with their sales office and their representative took me through some of the condo flats and town homes. The area was still under construction but finalized floor plans were on display and the houses and condos were all priced to sell fast. As our group walked into the last town house we looked at that day I knew that I had come home. It was absolutely beautiful! You know – corner unit, all windows and direct sunlight which I love. It had a decent sized kitchen with all new appliances, living area and half-bath downstairs. Upstairs had two spacious bedrooms, a lovely full bathroom next to the master bedroom and a laundry cabinet with plenty of storage and a new stack style washer and dryer. I have always been "laundry girl" and this would be my first experience having a washer and dryer of my own. The upstairs as well had lots of windows and lots of sunlight. I just wanted to pinch myself! We made an offer on the unit that day and waited for the paperwork to go through. Then I returned to my favorite penthouse apartment and began the process of packing boxes for the move.

Moving day came in June of 1999. Friends, family and the moving team started early in the morning and worked together to figure out how best to organize the furniture in the condo. Toward evening I was left alone to begin unpacking the maze of boxes and to put my bed together to sleep that night. I just looked at all the beauty around me and still could not believe it was mine. As He had promised, God truly had blessed me!

Room Mates and Kitties

As the summer of 1999 went on my little community was taking shape. Foundations were poured across the street for the first of over fifty single family homes which would be part of our neighborhood. Trees, shrubbery and flowers were planted and the area was looking really good. I had a few short-term room mates which offered some rent money to help with finances. My parents were still helping out some as I was balancing car debt, credit card debt and a mortgage on my income. It looked like finding the right room mate for the spare bedroom was the answer. My real estate agent had a daughter who went to my church and had been a close friend for many years. I remember walking through the new condo with him a number of times, and him saying to me "Now the master bedroom will be your bedroom". As we went into the spare bedroom he would say, "And this will be Laura's bedroom!" I heartily agreed. My friend, Laura, was sharing an apartment with her brother at the time. About one year after I moved into the townhouse, Laura's brother felt it was time for him to strike out on his own and she needed a place to live. I encouraged her to join me in my condo. We both prayed about it and in June of 2000 she became my room mate. She paid me monthly rent for use of the bedroom and condo and we shared paying the monthly bills. This was enough extra money for me to make it financially, and I no longer needed my parent's financial support. Thus began a friend and sister room mate relationship which lasted over nine years. It was truly a blessing from The Lord.

Another issue during that first year was adding the stress of being a new homeowner to the stress of learning a new computer system at work. The system we had would not take us through the Y2K issues which were right around the corner. I was asked to help with preparing and testing this new system and to help tailor it to the needs of our Department. I was also dealing with some emotional issues of this life, having survived a difficult childhood. The stress of this time both financial and emotional gave me a good case of IBS and I was sick for over a year from this. I had always internalized any kind of stress I was facing and it was time to find a new way to handle things. I had a pastor friend with a counseling ministry and signed up for some sessions with him. I found that it sometimes takes a real strength to see when you need help and reach out for it.

So I had to adjust from apartment life with people and noise all around me to life in a super quiet condo with few neighbors at first and not a lot of noise. I had wanted pets for years but could not make my desire for pets work with my apartment lifestyle. As a Condo owner I realized that I was now the landlord and getting a pet would bring a little more noise and a little more action around my home. This was confirmed when I helped care for a neighbor's cat which I called Abby. When it was time for Abby to go home again my home was way too quiet. Enter Ashie and Annie. I adopted them from a shelter at eight weeks old. They are sisters and have been my constant companions ever since. I had prayed to the Lord when picking them out for God's direction and that he would help me find the right ones. He truly did and my life would not be fully complete without them.

The Housewarming

About six moths after I moved into my home it was time to share with the rest of my world how God had blessed me. I invited everyone from my Church and a few friends from work to the housewarming. And what a party it was! I ended up having about fifty people come by and visit. Great people, great food, great times. My best friend showed up in the morning to help me prepare for the party, and people began to arrive early in the afternoon. Kitty Girls were securely sequestered in the spare bedroom and I only required them to make one appearance so I could show them off. Of course, they liked it better in the quiet bedroom upstairs.

As the day progressed it became time for some people to head home and the crowd began to thin out some. I was visiting with my friend, Chris and his young son by my front door when the unthinkable happened. I saw Chris lurch forward and say "Jared NO!...too late!" Before we could stop him little Jared had pulled the fire alarm handle by my front door. I guess the red lever that said "Pull Here" was just too tempting for him. Poor kid – he was really too little to realize what he was doing, and he was really embarrassed.

Well, everyone spilled outside onto the sidewalk as the alarm inside was deafening. I met quite a few of my neighbors that day. What an opportunity, right? I darted into my home long enough to grab my phone and then went back outside to call the emergency responders – to tell them that this was definitely <u>NOT</u> an emergency. I was still on the phone with the emergency dispatcher when the fire truck showed up. I felt so bad, and now little Jared was REALLY embarrassed. I apologized to the firemen and told them that a young guest at my housewarming had pulled the fire alarm.

So the challenge was for the firefighters to get into our cabana area so they could reset the alarm. Our Property Manager was having difficulty getting good cabana keys to the residents and none of us had access keys yet. As we stood around listening to the deafening alarm and wondering what to do the situation got worse. As we were trying to figure out access there was another fire truck screaming down the street – headed for a real incident. I wanted the ground to open up and swallow me about that time. The firefighters were not frustrated with me, but with the property manager. All the access keys should have been provided in the fire box before anyone was allowed to move onto the property. None of the keys were available and the Firefighters were missing a real call because of the lack of access. It was decided that the only remedy was for the firefighters to break into the cabana area so they could reset the alarm. One of the younger guys found a small window that was not locked and proceeded to crawl through head first, both legs sticking up in the air. I remember one of the women from my church saying she wanted to see that acrobatic trick again! Anyway, after crawling through the window he opened the cabana door so his team could enter and do their job. One more door to tackle, one more lock in the way. They had to use their axe to chop away at the door of the utility room where the fire alarm box was located. Those poor guys and their poor ears. The alarm was literally deafening in my condo, I can only imagine how loud it was in the cabana area. Finally to everyone's relief there was lovely silence.

Before the Fire Department left the scene, the Fire Chief had a chat with little Jared about the evils of pulling fire alarms. Jared was actually a pupil in my two and three year old Sunday School Class at the church. For the rest of that year every Sunday Morning Jared would say "Teacher, remember the day that I was at your house and I pulled the fire alarm?" I would always answer with great confidence, "Yes, Jared, I remember the day you pulled the fire alarm. And I will remember that day for many years to come!"

Problems in Paradise

———— ⚬ ————

So here I was, living my dream. I had a lovely home, wonderful kitty girls and a good job, and the best room mate in the world! Laura and I were loving our time together at church and at home. We had worked out a system where we had enough privacy but also enjoyed coming together for great conversation as well. We each organized our own meals and shared cupboard and fridge space in the kitchen. I definitely loved using all my shiny new appliances.

Things started to change in my community about five years after it was built. People's decks were beginning to show signs of wood rot and there was new evidence that the wood under the vinyl siding on all our buildings had not been treated properly. Within the next year my Condo neighborhood found itself in the middle of a construction defects crisis. Ours was not an unusual problem for the early years of this millennium – too many large building companies building too fast, cutting too many corners and then quickly moving on to their next building project.

Our Condo Board President along with the rest of the Condo Board went to work on this issue. The builder was prepared to leave this problem in the lap of his insurance company to deal with but our board President would not hear of this. She intended to hold this builder's feet to the fire and force him to send his own people out to our community and fix what unsupervised subcontractors working for his company had done, making things right on his company's dime. She had even had an employee of this building company come to some of our board meetings to discuss the reconstruction plans. Unfortunately, within the year this Condo Board President got married and moved out of the community.

Another President took her place that had a different vision of how to tackle this situation. She brought in an attorney who also had some construction experience as well. This seemed to be a good idea at first. As time went on it became apparent that this attorney had a reputation of unethical practices and many relationships that appeared to be conflicts of interest. Our Condo Board under the leadership of this new president also organized homeowner meetings which were really too early for most working people who commute to attend them, and then stopped communicating effectively with the homeowners group. It seemed like this circle of people in charge were all covering for each other and we had a Condo Board gone rogue. Looking back now it seems like maybe this Board got themselves into a situation that later they could not get themselves out of. The book of Ecclesiastes 8:12 in God's Word says "Though a sinner does evil a hundred times, and his days are prolonged, yet surely I know that it shall be well with them that fear God".

This attorney then began a legal battle against the builder's insurance company that went on for many years. In the mean time our community needed to begin fixing the construction problems. A decision was made by the Condo Board and the Property Management Company to organize special assessments for each homeowner to begin to pay for the work of rebuilding our homes. These assessments added up to anywhere between $22,000 and $28,000 per homeowner. We were offered loans organized by the Condo Board and the Property Management Company from a bank that they had been in contact with. Unfortunately by this time the amount of trust we had in this Condo Board and the attorney they had hired was extremely low. Those of us who could went to our Mortgage carriers and were able to get home equity loans to cover this expense. Many homeowners did not have equity to cover this and so they chose to go with the bank financing that the Condo Board offered. Many homeowners could not afford this expense. Some marriages did not last because of the financial stress. Some homeowners were forced into foreclosure over this. It seemed like an extreme nightmare – but it was about to get worse.

Our attorney suggested a reconstruction company that had a reputation of picking up unemployed people who needed work and teaching them a trade. This was a great thing in theory, but we ended up with about eighty percent of the construction workers fixing our defect problems completely untrained. A number of them had never held a hammer before. These guys were rebuilding our decks, treating the wood under our vinyl siding and replacing rotting stairwells because the wood in the initial construction had not been treated properly. The Construction Supervisors were constantly running from worker to worker showing them how to do the job.

My building was the first one to be fixed for this project and it literally took forever. I guess it was the guinea pig for the workers to learn what would work and what would not. The entire project was set to take six months, and it ended up taking a total of eighteen months. As time went on our attorney was in and out of court with our case and when we lost the case he appealed to the Supreme Court. More time paying attorney fees and managing huge debt. But what I found out later was that God truly had a plan for me in this difficulty.

Over time we were able to change to a different Condo Board and make some changes to help our community heal. But as I said before it was many years before movement came in our legal case and this nightmare would come to an end.

Church Transition

My church was truly my refuge. It was where my friends were and what my life revolved around. Each season there brought new joys, celebrations and challenges. I go into depth in my first book *Life Overcomer* about my completely broken state when I first started going there and recommitted my life to Christ. That wonderful group of people worked hard to put me back together and held my hand as I learned how to walk in Christ and gained strength. I truly loved my Pastors. They had taken me in as a daughter and had really seen me through a lot in life. If I had my way I would have stayed there the rest of my life. I really felt in some ways that I owed my life to that church and its people. But God had another plan for me. My Senior Pastor who had started the church many years earlier was ready to retire and when he did things started to go bad.

The man who had been chosen to take his place had been a youth camp speaker for our church in the past and I had a lot of respect for him. The first year he took over as Pastor went alright. There were a few red flags but no blaring warning signs yet. The man did have a prophetic ministry in the Lord. As time went on there was more of a spirit of pride that took over, and he truly felt and preached like he was God's prophet for God's hour. It really caused a lot of turmoil. People did start to walk away from the church and find other places of worship, but this place was my home. I was not ready to give up on it yet. I was still involved with children's ministry and spent a lot of time with the children. It was a real concern for me that there was not a safe, secure place for the kids to hang out after service and many times they ended up running around the church parking lot. This was a real tragedy ready to happen as mostly these kids were unsupervised and their Parents were still visiting.

Through a friend who worked for the city of Mountlake Terrace we were offered some commercial playground equipment for free, as a city park was getting new playground equipment. All we needed to do was to haul it onto our church grounds and build a fence around it. Problem solved right? Not so fast! Apparently this new pastor took issue with the fact that he was not the first one approached with this offer so he turned it down. I was devastated for those children. All I wanted to find out was what had happened. I tried to ask the Pastor about it. I tried to ask a few Church Board Members. No one wanted to talk about it. That dream had to die. The more I watched this new Pastor the more I saw deception. I would just be chatting with him and I knew that he was being deceptive with me. Over the next year his messages got farther from God's word and more toward the idea that he was God's Anointed Prophet and how he had no one to answer to but God. Well, in many ways this was true (the second part, not the first)! I ended up burying myself more and more into the Children's Church ministry so that I did not have to listen to him preach. I remember waking up on Sunday mornings with real dread in my heart and knots in my stomach anticipating the conflict I was to face that day. All I can say is that when you wake up on Sunday morning with that kind of dread in your heart it's time to think about moving on. But leaving my church would be leaving the main source of support in my life. I just didn't see how I could break free.

During this time some friends who were also having serious problems dealing with where the church was heading began attending another larger church in Bothell, Washington which was holding services on Saturday nights. This was giving them the shot in the arm they needed to deal with the conflict they faced on Sunday mornings. One weekend I asked if I could join them. It was the first weekend in September and the Pastor of this church had a great appreciation and burden for teachers. Each September he would ask the teachers and school administrators to stand up and he would pray a blessing over them for the upcoming school year. Well, the first service I attended there was Teachers weekend. I stood for prayer when asked because of my administrative job at my University. After this Pastor finished praying for us all, he looked right at me and said "I will be praying for you this week". This man had never seen me before in his life, and had no idea how much I needed his prayers. But God did. I remember thinking "I love this Man"! I knew that I would be back.

The more I prayed about God's plan for me, the more I knew that God was moving me on. By this time I had completely buried myself in Children's Church on Sunday mornings, making preparations for my final Christmas play at the church. Part of my heart was breaking for the children I knew I would be leaving, and the other part of my heart felt relief and anticipation for the wonderful, safe environment I would soon enter to worship Christ and receive encouragement. Many times when churches experience these challenges they end up in a church split, where a nucleus of people exit and start another church. What was being experienced with this situation was more like a sheep scatter – wounded sheep, or God's people, running for cover and looking for a safe refuge. By the end of December the Christmas Play was behind me, tearful goodbyes were said and I knew it was time to go.

In January I entered into my new spiritual home. I was battered, bruised, sad and extremely lonely. I had walked away from the church I had loved and served for 26 years and I was alone, and entering into a large church where I knew no one. It was excruciating. But I trusted my new Pastor and his knowledge of God's word. I also walked into this new church with the knowledge that God had called me there. I remember seeing a small church choir being invited a few times to lead worship for the church services and it being a joyous, uplifting experience. I remember thinking "I want to do that"! I saw a notice in the church bulletin that January saying that choir rehearsals for Easter were beginning and to contact the choir director if you were interested. No auditions necessary – just a love of singing. I joined the choir the next week. I also wanted to volunteer with the children and help lead Kids Worship. I signed up for this as well and went through the required background checks. My involvement with the choir and the kids helped me to meet people and create new friendships, many that remain important to me today.

That first year at this new church was a time of real growth and soul searching for me. My previous church was the only real exposure I'd ever had to God's word. Even though they had done many things right, there were some doctrines which were out in left field. I spent that first year asking myself "Why do I believe what I believe?" and making the foundations of my faith more secure. The next year my new Pastor did a sermon series of messages on the foundations of our faith, and these messages served to reinforce the changes I had made.

It took one more year for my former church to finally implode. The friends that I left there walked away from this church as well and found new places to worship. At times I am still sad when I think of all the great years I spent there and what that place had meant to me. But I am also very thankful that these friends of mine and I have found safe, wonderful places to worship where God's word is preached in truth.

Disability

As these things were going on at home and at my church, I found that physical changes were happening to me at work. One issue was that the corrective knee surgeries I had during my teen years were coming back to bite me. What I found out later is that one thing they used to do back in the 1970's to correct dislocating knee caps was to move the knee higher in the socket so that it was physically impossible for them to dislocate. I had this done to both my knees at age fifteen. No wonder I had issues with stairs – my knee caps were hitting wrong!

I was also having challenges with Carpel Tunnel Syndrome after more than twenty years of power style data entry on the job. So add to this an ankle injury from missing a step at my former apartment, back issues from falling from a grandstand at a Christian Music Weekend event (not one of my more graceful moments) and shoulder issues. Ok, so my body was getting older. Part of it too is that when you have some physical challenges you depend a lot more on your hands to get around. I went to visit specialists and went for x-rays. The x-ray techs would ask me what I did for a living. When I told them they would just shake their heads. One specialist after examining me talked to me about my job and told me that my hands and the tendons in my arms were showing signs of wear. I possibly needed to think about a different career. So I invested in wrist splints for work, driving and sleeping. I also made the difficult decision to give up playing my guitar which was a huge part of my life. I wanted to save my hands for the job. I hoped this would buy me some time to figure out what I wanted to do in my next career. Time went on and I had been praying about my future and my hands. They did show some improvement and the wrist splints went into the desk drawer.

Another issue was that sometimes I had dizzy spells or Vertigo. I was trying to manage this as well. I remember in March of 2007 I was enjoying a week of storm watching on the Oregon coast. I was a slower walker because of my physical challenges so I picked up my pace to try and catch up to the gang. All of the sudden my knees gave out. I was in too much pain to take another step without help and my friends helped me back into our hotel room. I was really upset and scared. The truth that my physical challenges were worse than I realized was beginning to dawn on me. I hung around the hotel for the rest of the trip, and tried to pace myself whenever I went out.

My hands were also acting up again and my Human Resources Department got involved this time. They worked with my new Specialist to get a Labor and Industries claim started. Human Resources also brought in a consultant to work with me and my department to assess my job and my challenges. One of the big issues was that the office I worked in did not have handicap access, and my job still had quite a bit of data entry involved. This consultant's report stated that I could not spend much more time doing this job. I was referred to an Orthopedic Surgeon for my wrists and I began to plan for Carpel Tunnel surgery. I spoke with this surgeon about my job and his prescription for me was "no more repetitive motion bilateral hands". I went home and called my supervisor to share this news, and I was officially on Labor and Industries Time Loss. I never was able to go back to that job.

Surgery on the left wrist was scheduled for August, 2007. After giving the wrist time to heal I began a regiment of occupational therapy to strengthen me and to learn to use my left hand and wrist again. I also had conversations with the therapist on what I should be doing going forward from here. We decided that data entry would not be part of the plan. The right wrist did not show the same amount of damage as the left one had during testing so Labor and Industries would not approve the surgery for the right wrist. I came to believe that this was for the best. It was my primary hand and I felt that the surgery I did have on the left side didn't really benefit me that much. My problems were way beyond Carpel Tunnel Syndrome.

Seeing that I could no longer do the job I had been doing for the last fourteen years I applied for several other jobs on my University Campus as they became open. I made sure that they were accessible for me with my physical challenges and that there would not be excessive data entry or typing. I was always praying that God would have his way, and if this was not His plan for me that He would block the application. This is just what He did. The friends who really knew me were becoming concerned about this. They believed that the disability issues I faced would not support full time work any more. But I was not willing to accept this. I had to keep trying.

There was another, deeper issue I was dealing with as well. There were so many parallels between what was happening to me physically during this time and what had happened to me growing up. Here I was dealing with a lot of pain, no real direction and no answers. I remember wishing after I had come to Christ that I had found Christ as a child, that the great challenges I had faced would have been easier as I would have learned how to handle them better. I guess this falls under the category be careful what you wish for! I remember having a Choir Weekend at the new Church and the Choir Director felt like I should share a testimony. The song I was to share around was "Your Grace is Enough. Great is your faithfulness, O God. You use the weak to lead the strong. You lead us by still waters into mercy, and nothing can keep us apart. So remember your promise, O God." I shared what was happening with me, my latest challenges and the parallels with what I was going through now and what I had faced growing up. I said that there was a whole new dynamic of peace and calling, even though I really didn't know what was coming next. There was not a dry eye in my Choir, or in the congregation.

By November of 2007 my University's Family Medical Leave policy could not carry me any longer and

I was invited to come in to Human Resources for an exit interview. That was a very sad day for me after twenty six years working there. I knew that I could not go back to my former position and nothing else had opened up. Fortunately, my University had invested in Long Term Disability Insurance for me and I was encouraged to apply for it. I did and my case was accepted. This, I thought, would be great for the interim between jobs and while I healed from my injuries. It was going to be short term anyway. So I thought.

I kept checking the University website for open positions and hunted online for jobs as well. I was determined to get myself back into the workforce. I saw a job posting in February of 2008 which looked interesting. My University's Nursing School was looking for someone to work eight hours per week. I felt funny applying for something with so few hours but I felt the Lord encourage me to apply. Maybe it would at least get my foot back in the door on my Campus. I interviewed and was offered the job. Maybe over time it would work into more hours, right? I loved my new Department and the work I did there. I started doing two four hour shifts per week, something my Doctors and Human Resources felt I could physically handle. Soon after taking the job I had the opportunity to work up to twenty hours per week to fill in for a workmate who was going to be having surgery. Three weeks later my wrist issues were out of control again. Denial was over. I had to come to terms with the fact that I was truly disabled. My long term disability pension did allow me to work part time so I scaled back to my two short shifts again when my friend returned to work after her surgery. I spent time praying about what God wanted me to do. He let me know that he was in this, He loved me and was for me. His plan for me was for me to take care of myself and be committed to my physical therapy routine, my quiet time with him and to pray for and spend time with my family. This would be my new calling in Him. I did my best to keep up my end of the bargain, and felt his blessing as I did.

Mediation

—— ⏱ ——

With my wrists re-injured and with the encouragement of my Human Resources Department I went back to visit the Orthopedic Surgeon who had operated on my wrist the year before. He looked at me and at my wrist, and said "You've had your surgery and time off work. You are all healed up now." Poor man – he really didn't know what to do with me! We opened a new Labor and Industries Claim and I could feel their disbelief – injured at work at a job contracted for eight hours per week. How pathetic is that!

My favorite Nurse Practitioner referred me to a hand specialist in a Seattle Clinic. This place had special technology and one of those computer programs that can magnify x-rays into images large enough to tell what's really going on. What they could see was a mixture of bone, nerve and tendon issues brought on by over use. My hands truly were falling apart. There was a hand specialist there at this clinic who had a lot of experience working with Labor and Industries. I began to see this doctor who was invaluable in the Labor and Industries process. The next six months were filled with letters going back and forth between me and my Labor and Industries Claims Manager who was convinced that I could not possibly have been re-injured at a job working only eight hours per week.

It is the job of the injured person and their Medical Team to provide Labor and Industries with the burden of proof of injury, medical evidence. This can be really challenging and the communications between my Claims Manager and I were growing more combative. Even with the medical evidence I had of my injuries and letters from this Doctor I was getting nowhere with him. I did get a referral to a Disability Attorney and talked with his office several times. They never did take my case but the advice they gave me over the phone was helpful to get me through this process. I came to see it in the end as free legal advice, a real blessing. I really did feel like little David against big Goliath.

I found out in the Winter of 2009 that Labor and Industries was sending my case into mediation. This is a situation where everyone in the process is represented by an attorney – except the injured person. Fair fight? Not! This is a less expensive way, though, to get you claim taken care of than investing in a disability attorney. These mediation meetings were attended by a Labor and Industries attorney, an attorney representing the employer sometimes by teleconference, the injured person and a friend or family member, and a mediator. Walking into these meetings can really make you feel like everything is stacked against you. But we serve a mighty, powerful, glorious God and I knew that He was with me.

For my first mediation session I brought one of my good friends from my church. She had known me for thirty years and knew that I was honest and a hard worker. I remember the attorney from Labor and Industries reading the report from the surgeon who had operated on my wrist which said that things were fixed. This attorney referred to the surgeon as a "wrist specialist". But I knew better. "No, I said, this doctor is not a wrist specialist, he is an orthopedic surgeon. My friend here's mother broke her ankle last year and this doctor operated to fix it. The doctor I have now, whose medical reports you have, is an actual wrist specialist." My specialist's medical evidence trumped the first orthopedic surgeon's statement and I knew it. This attorney looked extremely unhappy with my statement, but my friend was there to verify it.

I attended five more mediation sessions and after each session I was sent back to my Specialist for more medical evidence, or to retract what Labor and Industries was now saying. The whole mediation process took about one year. Each appointment I made with this Specialist was not covered by Labor and Industries and needed to be paid for out of pocket, with the possibility of being reimbursed after the mediation process was over. Sometimes my Dad would come to these mediation meetings with me, sometimes another friend would come with me for moral support. I remember many times the night before these mediation meetings I would lie awake and be filled with dread and fear. But the Lord would speak peace to my heart and encourage me, and let me know that he was with me in this fight.

Also during this time things were changing around my home. My room-mate ended up without a job about six months after I went on Labor and Industries in 2007. She had enough money saved to float her for a year while she hunted for another job, but by now the economy had hit the skids along with the job market. She was running out of money. About the same time we heard from our condo board that the Insurance Company involved in our construction defects case had offered to settle with another community. We were able to bring a different, better attorney into this process and approached this Insurance Company about settling. And it worked! The same week I lost my room mate I was able to pick up a check to reimburse me for the entire amount of the Special Assessment I had paid all those years ago. God indeed had a plan through all the drama that had happened. I kept the money in savings to pay the medical bills during the mediation process and when it was over I was able to pay off the loan I took out over the assessments.

In time Labor and Industries had to finally concede that, at last, I really was injured and prepared to offer me a payout. The mediation team needed a few more weeks to work out the particulars of my case. When I asked if I needed one more appointment with my wrist specialist to obtain the information they needed, the answer was a resounding "NO!" Apparently Labor and Industries did not want to reimburse me for any more doctor visits. I was told that the procedure was for Labor and Industries to make me a settlement offer and wait for my response. What actually happened was this. My Claims Manager was so angry with the decision Labor and Industries had come to that he just sent me a small check along with a letter stating in all caps "THIS CLAIM IS CLOSED!" Fine with me! When my Dad asked how I felt about how things had worked out I had only two words to say. "We Win!"

Mom's Time

*s I entered into my Fiftieth year I began to deal with an issue that many people my age are dealing with – that of aging parents. I loved my Mother dearly and growing up she was my constant companion and my best friend. Even after I left home and started my career I would still call her every day to touch base, but when I came to Christ this began to change. The closer I came to The Lord and the more I built the foundation of my life on God's Word the larger the gulf between my mother and I grew. It was like we were living in two different worlds, and in many ways we were. My Mom told me later that at first she was angry and resentful about this change in my heart and my belief system and the time I was spending at the church and with my new friends. Over the years her perspective did change and she was able to see the growth in me as a person, and the good things God was doing in me.

The thing that affected our relationship the most was that my Mom could never get past the fact that I still struggled with weight issues, and needed to lose weight. This was my age-old problem. I desperately wanted her support in all the things in my life that were going right, but it seemed all she could see was the one area of my life where I struggled. I do have a family member who has struggles with mental illness and eating disorders. The eating disorder has many times been life threatening, but by the Grace of God and the prayers of God's people this family member is still with us. I remember seeing my parents after they had been away fishing or at their winter home in Palm Desert and dreading seeing my Mom again, knowing that an intervention meeting would be coming. I didn't understand why she could ignore the dangerous eating disorder affecting this close family member but could not see me past my weight challenges. This was a double-standard to me.

By the time I reached my fifties our relationship was miles apart and in need of serious healing. I was also noticing that my Mom was beginning to look frail. She had back injuries one summer which led to significant weight loss because of the pain she was in, weight that she could not really afford to lose. She never did return to a normal weight. Mom had always been so strong, so determined, never letting anything get in her way or slow her down. I never did see a time when she just sat, even long enough to watch a movie with us. She always had to be up doing something for the family she loved.

Things started to really change for her in 2009. She lost interest in a lot of her former passions such as playing bridge, reading, cooking, and boating. She was tired and just wanted to rest. Also about this time I started noticing signs of memory loss. Mail was being lost and bills were not paid. This was something that was really scary for her as she had always been so strong and independent. One way I kept our relationship going was to do some light bookkeeping and paperwork for her. When Mom began to have more time challenges I offered to step in for laundry duty and ironing Dad's shirts. It was a true labor of love and I was glad to help. My Dad worked with her to eat more and put on some weight. He also would sit at her elbow and they worked together on their personal finance paperwork to get their bills paid. He was so patient with her! Over time I noticed with the paperwork I was doing for them that Mom's handwriting was almost illegible and really shaky. The next month the handwriting was Dad's. She never did go back to do those books again.

I remember many warning signs I saw that hit me very hard. One time I was having a lovely dinner with my parents and my sister at their Country Club. This was our favorite place to get together and celebrate. It had marvelous food and a beautiful view of Lake Washington. As we got up to leave the table Mom was suddenly unable to walk. She was literally paralyzed with fear. After some coaxing and some help Mom was able to make it to a chair where she could sit down and rest. After a while and some help from Dad and Sis she was able to get up, into the car and home. I cried all the way home that night and cried myself to sleep. I remembered with my grandmother when life changes happened that were irreversible and I knew now with my Mom that there was no going back to healthier, happier days. Dad ordered her a walker with a seat on it for her to sit if she got too tired to walk. It was also really difficult to get her off the couch when she was resting, sometimes taking two or three people to get her standing. A few times Dad even had to call the medics to help get her into bed. Then the falls began. Trips to the Hospital, then to Assisted Living until she was strong enough to return home – only to fall again.

It was during this period of time that I felt The Lord impress on my heart that I should start reading to Mom. I asked my Dad about this and he thought it would be a great idea. So I would come over to the house or to the Rehab Facility a few times a week and read to her for a while. My Mom's favorite books were fiction novels based on history. As we went through these books it began to bridge the gap between us. This was not always easy, though. I had severe learning disabilities growing up, and one of the hardest things for me to do was to read aloud. Sometimes I would read a sentence and Mom would say "Wait, I didn't understand that part." So I would go back and read it again, working it out. This was such a sweet time shared between us.

By 2011 the walker was replaced by a wheelchair. Mom had been diagnosed with a form of dementia. One of the ways the dementia manifested was that it robbed her of her appetite. Dad did a beautiful job taking care of her. I watched him transform from a strong, independent guy who loved to golf into a patient caregiver, giving up his own life to care for his wife. After another fall Mom was spending more time in the hospital to heal from her injuries. I had been concerned for years about my parents and their spiritual condition, and had shared on many occasions what God had done in my life. As I was heading out to visit her this day I felt that The Lord wanted me to share a simple message of God's love with her. As divine providence would have it, I had some time alone with her. In the middle of our visit I told her "Mom, I want you to know that God can help you with this struggle. All you need to do is to ask Him. It's not a big hard thing, it's easy. Just ask The Lord to help you." She looked at me and said "Thank You." I believe that it took this great struggle to bring her to a place where she could receive these words. I knew just a few years earlier she would not have been ready to hear it. I felt I could now release her to The Lord with confidence. It was the job of the Holy Spirit to draw her to Christ. I knew that with what I had shared with her in the past and her own knowledge of the Christian Faith that her heart had been prepared for that specific moment. She was ready.

Dad now came to realize that the family home was no longer a safe place for them to live so arrangements were made to move her to an Assisted Living Facility where he could get more help with her care. He then began preparations to put our family home up for sale. This was such a hard decision for the entire family. This house had been built to my Mom's specific specifications and was their dream house. It had a view of Lake Washington like I have never seen before and our family had lived there since I was four years old. What a blessing to grow up around such beauty! But the property taxes had become too much to handle and the upkeep of the home too much work. It was time to let it go. And wouldn't you know – The perfect buyer came at just the right time. Dad had arranged an estate sale and the company brought in to help with it sent out advertisements to invite the community. This couple with a young family came to the estate sale to check it out, fell in love with the house and the view, and made an offer on the spot! It was now their turn to love, care for and enjoy this home that we had loved and lived in for over fifty years.

As Mom's health declined and Dad could no longer leave her alone he asked me to step in more and more to spell him off so he could run errands and do what he needed to do. By now I was doing the grocery shopping for him so he didn't need to worry about that. So Mom and I read books together and watched our favorite movies. This time spent together just the two of us did the work of bringing a final healing touch to our relationship. I remember the last book I read to her. It was about a young missionary girl to Hawaii and was literally packed with encouraging scripture. Mom absolutely loved it! I had been waiting my entire adult life for this moment – being able to genuinely share my heart and my faith with my mother and feel that connection. I thank The Lord every day that he gave us this time to spend together.

I received a call from Dad on Friday Evening, December 30, 2011 that Mom was on the way to the Emergency Room. She had collapsed in the middle of dinner and was not breathing on her own. When I met Dad at the Emergency Room they had her on a breathing tube and she was in distress. They had to strap her wrists onto the sides of her bed to keep her from trying to pull the breathing tube out. Poor Mom, she did not understand that the breathing tube was her lifeline. It was so hard! The family kept vigil the entire weekend, and on the afternoon of January 1st, 2012, she gave up her fight. She was just short of 86 years old and went to Heaven peacefully surrounded by the family she had spent her whole life caring for. I remember that the exact moment she passed away I felt the weight of the world lift from off my shoulders and I was filled with God's peace. I knew she had made it to heaven!

We had a small memorial service for her which my Dad organized and officiated and my brother, my cousin and I spoke at the service. I talked about the love my parents had for each other and told a funny story about how they met. I thanked my Dad for taking such good care of her in front of all their friends who were there. I told the crowd there that I viewed death in Christ not as the end, but as a graduation into something more wonderful and glorious than we could imagine. I talked about how I had come home from the Hospital after Mom died and picked up a daily devotional I had just received from a good friend – a birthday present. That January 1st devotion talked about how we learn things from other people every day – things to do and things not to do. The devotional question was this. What did you learn from someone else today? Here is what I wrote and shared.

Things I learned from my Mother's life

Love Always
Forgive Forever
Stay Positive
Love People
Be Friendly
Make the Best of Each Day
Keep Marriage Strong
Love Life
Have Fun
Do Something Nice for Someone Else
Keep Loved Ones Near
I love you, Mommy. I'll miss you
forever. Happy Graduation Day!

Cancer

Life after Mom's passing was really busy and I was watching Dad pretty close, long laundry for him and keeping him in groceries and supplies. My goal was to see him through this first year after Mom's passing. They had been married for 59 years and I knew he was lonely. I missed Mom so much but was happy that her struggle with life and pain was over and that she was safely home with Jesus. Life consisted of doing my physical therapy homework, my part time job, looking after Dad and spending time with my brother and his wife. It was in the middle of the process of grieving my Mom that I suddenly was thrust from grief into survival mode. I went for my yearly mammogram in mid-July, 2012, and the clinic saw something in the images that they were unsure of. They wanted me to come back in for further scans. I remember the moment I hung up the phone that day I knew that I was going to be fine. I responded saying, "Yes, I'm going to be fine." I went back the following Monday for the extra scans and the results were still inconclusive. I was signed up for a needle biopsy on that Friday. The

middle of the next week the answer came. I was given
the diagnosis of Ductile Carcinoma in my left breast,
both semi-aggressive and aggressive. I was on the phone
immediately with a surgeon's office I had been referred to
by the clinic I had originally gone to. I then started the
difficult process of informing my family, co-workers and
friends that I had cancer. Thus began a journey to regain
my health and my life that would take the next year.

I remember my initial reaction to this diagnosis was
anger directed toward this disease. How dare it attack me!
No one invited it to the party of my life and my goal was
to make this cancer sorry that it had chosen to attack my
body. To squish it like a tiny little bug.

I found a surgeon I liked at the office I was referred
to. This woman became head of a team of doctors for
phase one of treatment which included special MRI scans
to identify the cancerous area, the surgery to remove
the cancer and planning for reconstruction surgery.
After conversations with this surgeon I opted for a breast
reduction on both breasts in lieu of reconstruction. This
is something I had wanted to do for many years. I also
chose to wait for this breast reduction until all cancer
treatment was over. I could see it as my reward for going
through the torture of the treatment! In August I had
a lumpectomy surgery on my left breast and ended up
loosing about half of it. As protocol they removed the
two sentinel lymph nodes on that side and when tested
they did show signs of cancer. The surgeon then removed
six more lymph nodes which were clear. The next day I
was joined in my Hospital room by my best friend and
my brother who wanted to meet with the Surgeon and

discuss where to go from here. This surgeon had been in discussion with her medical team. They had definitely found more cancer than they thought there was. Since this cancer had begun to spread to my lymph nodes she felt that the best treatment plan for me to keep the cancer from returning would be to put me though eight rounds of chemotherapy, then radiation after that. This was the first time chemo was added to the conversation and I was less than thrilled. I had been planning to be done with treatment by Christmas, now with chemo in the mix I would be in treatment until the following summer. There was one more day surgery planned for September to insert a Port-A-Cath which would facilitate my chemotherapy treatments. Until now this whole experience seemed surreal, like I was watching it happen to someone else. Now, looking chemotherapy square in the face it was very real and it did not look like fun. But if it would squash the cancer I was willing to walk through this experience one day at a time, holding my Lord's hand.

Chemotherapy started in early October of 2012. I walked into it really nervous, not knowing what to expect. I received my first A/C infusion at a Hospital in Edmonds, Washington and immediately struck up a friendship with the nurses there. Jeannie and Sarah became confidants and were great to advise me and answer questions during my four hour visits. Chemo has really changed over the years to become more tolerable for its patients. One thing they do now is to start you off with almost an hour of anti-nausea IV infusions before they introduce the actual chemotherapy drug. I also had filled a prescription for anti-nausea which I had at home. This combination of anti-nausea made the A/C infusions easier to deal with.

I had worked out with my part time job to change work days to Monday and Tuesday. Chemo day was every third Wednesday. I would usually be fine for the first two days after chemo then start to feel the effects of the poison either Friday or over the weekend. It was not unusual for me to miss the next week of work, then I would have two weeks where I felt ok. My best friend and I mapped out my chemotherapy schedule and put it on our calendars. We were excited to see that my treatment missed Thanksgiving, my Birthday Week and Christmas. What a blessing to have great friends to walk through this experience with me!

In visiting my Oncologist office for a blood draw two weeks after my first chemo my nurse encouraged me to set myself up with a wig as soon as I could. Hair loss usually starts between week three and four after beginning Chemotherapy. I was referred to a Cancer Resource Center in Everett, Washington and went to see them the next day. I had already gotten a short hair cut in anticipation of this hair loss. This Resource Center was able to supply me with a wig that really suited me and some knit hats at no charge to me. This was such a blessing! About one week later, just after my second chemotherapy infusion the hair started coming out. I noticed it first as I was washing my hair, it was coming out in fistfuls. Another thing I noticed was that my scalp was getting extremely tender and painful. Just laying my head on the pillow at night or feeling my hair blow in the wind was extremely painful. I knew that it was time for the hair to go. I visited my hairdresser and had a long talk with her. She knew about my diagnosis and had been praying for me. As my friend, she was committed to taking care of me. I told her a funny story about the wife of a boss I had worked for who had also gone through breast cancer, and how they had made the shaving of her head a fun family event. Apparently when her head was half shaved they stopped for photos! When my hairdresser heard this story, she said "That's It! I'm giving you a Mohawk and we're taking pictures!" And that was what we did. Even topping the Mohawk off with the red hair dye on the top. She took a few pictures of me with my cell phone. Then before she finished shaving my head, she shaved everything except for the front lock of my bangs and said "And now this is how you would look with a comb over." I now have a permanent record of my special hairdo and it was really funny to pull out my phone and show friends and family who were supporting me through this. The wig I received looked enough like my natural hair that most people didn't know it was a wig unless I revealed my secret. It really worked out well. It took a few weeks but I became accustomed to seeing myself without hair on my head, without eye lashes and eyebrows. I felt I could go bald around the house and I would either go for the wig or for a knit hat when I went out during the winter months. My morning devotional routine was a great comfort to me during this time. There is a song written back in the 1980's around Psalm 5:1-3. It says "Give ear to my prayer O Lord, consider my meditation. Hearken unto the voice of my cry, my King and my God. For unto thee will I pray; my voice will thou hear in the morning. O Lord, in the morning will I direct my prayer unto thee and will look up." It truly gave me the knowledge that God truly knew what I was going through and gave me peace.

Thanksgiving was great. I spent time with my best friend and her family, the nucleus of my Christian family. I was recovered enough from chemo to enjoy some food, though I was having some food association issues and my appetite was getting smaller. Then I went to join my Dad at my brother's house for Thanksgiving Dinner. Christmas was spent with my Christian family in Bellingham, My wonderful hostess fills her home with snowmen each Christmas and each year her home is my winder wonderland. She surprised me on Christmas morning with an enormous Christmas stocking full of supplies – one of them a beautiful lightweight knit hat which was perfect for covering my baldness inside the house. It was an absolute Godsend! We had a wonderful, riotous time watching the now grown nieces and nephews open their Christmas treasures. We enjoyed great food and great times. The best part of all as that I was set to have my last A/C chemotherapy infusion the next week. I was going to be half way through this chemotherapy journey and the second chemo drug was supposed to be easier to handle and gentler. New Years Day was spent at my Brothers home to celebrate the holiday, visit with relatives and commemorate one year anniversary of Mom's passing. It was a great day of food, football and fun.

That weekend at church we had our yearly "Dear Jesus" letter which we wrote the first weekend of every year. We always write what we feel the next year will bring and share prayers for what God will do. This letter is then mailed home to us at the end of spring and we are able to read what we had written and what we were praying about, seeing what God had done. I had written that I was thankful that I was being switched to this new chemotherapy treatment that would be easier to tolerate. So I thought.

Taxitere and Me

---○---

$\mathcal{T}$axitere was the chemotherapy drug that had been scheduled for my final four infusions. My oncologist warned me before hand that sometimes his patients have a more severe reaction after their first infusion of this drug as there was still some A/C chemo in their system. One nice thing about Taxitere was that it did not have the stomach sensitivity issues that the A/C did. I had already been investing in aloe vera juice which I mixed with grape juice concentrate to keep my tummy feeling half decent and I continued to do this during my time on Taxitere. One drawback of this drug was that it caused severe joint pain. I already had joint issues from before, and I found that I needed pain medication for about five days after each infusion until this side effect wore off. Another thing was that as this chemo drug built up in my bloodstream my heart rate was beginning to spike dramatically. I noticed this most after I walked up the stairs of my townhouse. I would have to lie down on my bed for five minutes until my heart stopped pounding in my ears. This began to really concern me. By the time

I had my third Taxitere infusion in February of 2013 I was becoming really ill. I was eating and drinking all I could, but the chemo was making me secrete more water than I was taking in. I was also extremely weak and was spending more and more time in my bed. I felt like my body was starting to atrify. I knew that I needed to move more so I just put the cassettes on that I do my physical therapy to, and I did what I could. If I was too weak to do it, that was OK. At least I was listening to encouraging music and moving a little bit. My heart rate was racing so much that I could not walk fifteen feet without it pounding in my ears. I called and talked to the Oncology Nurse and she had me come in for IV fluids. I ended up missing a full month of work because I was too weak to walk from my car to my office.

I also became too weak to grocery shop. Many friends and neighbors had offered me help during my illness. Asking for help was one of the hardest things I did. One of my friends from work offered groceries one week. I gave her my list and she dropped things by that evening. When I asked her what I owed her she would not take my money. What a sweetheart! There was also a few times when my brother stopped in with fresh groceries and bags of cat litter. I felt truly blessed!

I learned to do things around me home a little bit at a time. Doing the cat box took three stints with rests in the middle. So did vacuuming my carpets upstairs. I would sit until my heart stopped pounding in my ears and then vacuum a little more. I also needed help from my neighbors to throw out my garbage as I was too weak to make it to the dumpster and back. If I were going to an appointment sometimes I would put my garbage in the trunk of my car, then back up next to the dumpster and throw the bags in. I felt like such a helpless twit!

Another side affect of the Taxitere is that it can cause fingernails and toenails to separate from the fingers and toes, putting them at risk for falling off. One way to keep this from happening was to put ice packs on both hands and feet while getting my infusion. This was really challenging. In the end I did end up keeping all my toenails, but did lose all my fingernails – one at a time.

By now I was one week away from my eighth and final chemotherapy infusion. I was really concerned because I knew that I would not be either physically or emotionally ready for it. I had been talking to with my brother and he was terribly concerned for me. He saw the neurological changes that the Taxitere was making for me and he was really afraid that some of these changes would not wear off completely. I was definitely having a strong adverse reaction to this poison that was coursing through my veins. I was seriously considering opting out of my final chemo. I knew after my surgery that the tissue taken out of my left breast was adequate and I had been told that my margins were clear. I definitely had a decision to make. I knew that as a single person living with my cats in a townhome the chemo had become a huge safety concern. I had come to the place where I could hardly walk or use my arms. My friends wanted me to come and stay with them but I wanted to manage on my own if I could. If I did walk through one more chemo infusion I thought a nursing home would be a better option! By the beginning of the next week my decision had been made.

I called and talked to my Oncology Nurse, telling her that I had decided to opt out of my final chemo. She wanted me to keep my Wednesday appointment and meet with the Oncologist. At this appointment we found that my sitting heart rate was slow and was hard to hear, and my blood pressure was extremely low as well. My standing heart rate and blood pressure were off the charts. I let this Doctor know that I was in no way strong enough to go through with another chemotherapy that day and that I had been having a severe reaction. I really wanted to opt out of my final treatment. He realized that I was also extremely dehydrated when he looked at my lab results and ordered more IV fluids for me. He said he wanted me to come back the following Wednesday and we could talk about what to do. His nurse helped me down the VERY LONG hall to their infusion room and I spent the next hour getting IV fluids. They wanted to see me again on Friday to check on me. I had another IV fluid infusion that Friday and then one the following Monday. Wednesday came and I met with the doctor again. He realized that I was indeed having a severe reaction and still suffering from dehydration. He said that most of his cancer patients were able to tolerate the full chemo regime, I was not one of those patients. So it was agreed. No more chemotherapy! I made my way down that long hall for one more batch of IV fluids before I headed home. I was so thankful for being done with the Taxitere. It was at least two more weeks before I could start back at my part time job. Even then I it was still really challenging to get from my car to my office and back. In time I could resume some of my normal activities like walking to the dumpster to take out garbage and grocery shopping. My friends and I had an April Alaska Cruise planned to celebrate getting through Chemo. We go every year and have learned to shop for bargain packages. Because of my cruise plans, radiation was put off a few extra weeks which was a relief to me. I felt like I had more of a chance to walk into radiation strong.

Radiation

———— ⊙ ————

$\mathcal{I}$t was wonderful spending a week with my great
travel buddies in Alaska. There is literally nothing
like experiencing the breathtaking beauty of the scenery,
great food and the fellowship of friends closest to you. I
was still dealing with lingering effects from chemotherapy
so I still had to pace myself. We shopped in the Alaskan
snow and wind and played our favorite games. It really
was a wonderful break from the reality which had become
my life.

I was scheduled the day of our return to Seattle for a
final set of scans before my first radiation appointment,
which would be the next day. These scans proved really
challenging for me. For the radiation procedure you
lay on your back on the radiation table, arms overhead
and hang onto the bars. My challenge was the position
my arms were in, resting midway in the air and I have
arthritic shoulders. They're really crunchy. It took the
technicians a little longer to find the perfect spots to tattoo
and treat me and I was not allowed to move. I was in so
much pain and in tears. I was really afraid of throwing

my shoulder. Unfortunately I was a little harsh with the technicians that day as they did not realize my challenges or the pain I was in. I had a long talk with the Oncology Nurse after this experience and that made me feel better. She explained that the actual process of radiation was much faster than the scans I had just undergone and that people with my shoulder challenges usually do better on the radiation table after a few days, and that my shoulders would loosen up.

All in all, radiation was a walk in the park compared to my chemo experience. My schedule for this radiation was five days a week, Monday through Friday for 6 ½ weeks – to be completed before the end of June. I scheduled my appointments for the afternoon so I could go to work or do my physical therapy in the mornings. I was supplied with aloe vera gel by the oncology office and used it a few times a day on the radiated area all through treatment and into the healing process.

In my second week of radiation I found that the rotating technicians were sometimes that of the male gender. This can lead to awkward moments especially if they were young and handsome, as they usually were. Here I was lying on a cold table, naked from the waist up except for a hand towel to cover my breasts. I just laid there and thought "I have now lost all dignity!" As I got to know these technicians I began to feel better about our daily visits. My time on the radiation table added up to about ten minutes and so I was usually heading back home within thirty minutes from when I arrived. I stayed after my treatments once a week to check in the Radiation oncology nurse and doctor, and so on doctor days my appointments were longer. They checked my skin on the radiated area and asked me how I was doing.

One side affect of the radiation treatments is fatigue, I found this manageable. I was thankful that my work hours were in the morning when I was fresh. After work I rested for an hour before my appointment. Sometimes the radiation appointment wore me out so I would lay down and rest after. It took about four weeks for my skin to begin to react from the treatment. I was getting what looked like a severe sunburn to the breast area and under my left arm. The aloe vera gel really helped keep the pain at bay. My left underarm was still numb from the lymph node surgery the year before and the technicians felt this was a blessing as this was the area which was burned the worst.

I also got to know some of the other patients as our appointments were next to each other. We compared notes about our experiences with chemo and radiation, and how it affected our lives. There was a bond growing between us and I looked forward to these visits.

Because of the Memorial Day Holiday and some equipment problems there were a few make up radiation days tagged on to the end of my treatment, but finally the day came – I walked out of the treatment room for the last time. I remember posting on Facebook "No more chemo, no more nukes. No more doctors prodding pokes. I was done! How I loved that word done. It took about four more weeks for my skin to heal completely. It reacted like a really bad sunburn, first tanning some, then peeling, with beautiful new skin underneath. I felt like I was getting my life back. I walked into my work the next day to a great surprise – a party! There was a sign posted on my office door and break room like a banner. It said "Daphne's to do list. Chemo (check) Radiation (check) Kick Cancer (check). There were brownies and homemade cookies to celebrate. It was so wonderful to celebrate with this group of co-workers who had supported me through this process. The Lord God had truly walked me through this past year one day at a time. And through the entire process I had the memory of the knowledge I had from day one that I was going to be fine. I had clung to this with all my strength through the hardest time, when the chemo had gotten really bad, and in my heart I knew that it was true. I was going to be fine. With the help of the Lord, my family and friends, the home group from my church and my amazing medical team and technicians, I had squashed this cancer like the tiny bug that it was. Psalm 118: 4-6 reads "Let those who fear the Lord say: His love endures forever. In my anguish I cried unto the Lord and he answered me by setting me free. The Lord is with me; I will not be afraid. What can man do to me?"

Restoration, Recovery and Beyond

I remember last December I was doing my devotional routine – time in the Word of God and journaling. As I was reading I felt like 2013 will be my year of restoration. 2012 had been such a challenging year with losing my Mother and then fighting cancer. I knew in December that I still had a battle to fight, but also that after treatment, healing would come.

One of the greatest victories through this cancer battle was financial. As a person on a small disability pension I could not afford to carry any debt if I wanted to stay in my home. I knew that God had made a way for me so far. One of my favorite promises from the Word is that God owns all the cattle on a thousand hills. I knew if need be, he could send one of those cows my way! I had a small savings account set aside, and a small medical reimbursement account set up by my company. I remember when the bills for my Chemo started to come in. I looked at the patient balance and knew I didn't have the funds to cover it. I also noticed a phone number to call to inquire about financial assistance. I called and talked to the hospital representative and he sent me a packet of information to fill out, along with a list of documents to send back with my application. After review, my application for financial assistance was accepted, with assistance up to 85 percent. I could have been carrying enough debt for my lifesaving treatment to be making payments for many years – but God came through. May God help me in the future to bless others the way this program has blessed me. The Lord also helped me so that every time a medical bill came in for surgery, doctor visits or treatment, there was money saved to pay it with. I have always been committed to giving my monthly tithe out of what little I had and supporting God's church. I know that God honors faithfulness. Those times when I needed help it was there for me.

Now here I am, more than half way through 2013, six months out from Chemo and two months out of radiation. My skin has healed completely, my fingernails are back and healthy again. My hair is growing and filling in thick. I have eyelashes again, the eyebrows are taking a little longer to return. The appetite affects of the Chemo are gone now, and the food association issues are pretty much gone. The feeling in my feet and toes are returning over time.

And now for the beyond. I have spent the last six years on disability of some type and honestly I have had a real problem with that. My personality type has always been industrious with a strong drive to make life better for me and for others. I have always had a passion for ministry, wanting my life to be an encouragement to others. Being on a disability pension can make you feel like you are stuck in a box, low income for the rest of your life with no chance to make things better. There were way too many "I can't do that any mores" in my life. I had been praying for the last six months about this to the Lord. "There must be something I can do to make things better" I felt so helpless, even though my needs were met I always hated being on public assistance. Recently my mind drifted to my first manuscript from 1998, **Life Overcomer**, a testament to what God has done in my life. Somehow in the midst of all my challenges, writing had always come easy for me. As I thought about this manuscript the day after Radiation ended, I sensed the voice of the Lord speak to me saying "Now here is something you can do"! I was immediately filled with joy and new purpose. One thing about me that was never affected by disability was the ability to talk – and I can do that a lot!

So it was time to give this first manuscript final edits, transfer it onto my current computer and look for God's direction in publishing. I also want to do some speaking about what God has done for me and be able to encourage others. I'd love for this new direction in my life to take me way past retirement and open many doors.

The story of my life is this – we serve an Awesome, Mighty, Powerful God who loves us, and longs for us to be in relationship with Him. In those life situations which seem too difficult to handle, He is there in the middle of them. When there seems to be no way out, He can show you the way. Jesus can give the courage to face the circumstances in life that seem impossible.

Just take his hand and let him walk you through. In the good times and the difficult times of this life, God's word is still as true and sure as ever. Jeremiah 29:11 "For I know the plans I have for you declares The Lord, plans to prosper you and not to harm you, plans to give you a hope and a future".

Printed in the United States
By Bookmasters